Trust It!

You Have the Power Within You

Mary Catherine Dalk

Trust It!

You Have the
Power Within You

MARY CATHERINE VOLK

All One World Books & Media

Print book ISBN: 978-1-945963-46-9
eBook ISBN: 978-1-945963-47-6

Cover photograph: Marco Island, Florida sunset by
Mary Catherine Volk

Published by All One World Books & Media,
Rhode Island, USA, all1world.com

Interior and cover design:
Ruth Shilling, ruthshilling.com

❦ ❧ ❦ ❧

This book is dedicated to
my beloved husband, Rick.
You always supported me in my
many endeavors and I know you
continue to do so from
the world of spirit.

❦ ❧ ❦ ❧

Table of Contents

Introduction

What makes you happy? What brings you joy on a daily basis? What lights up your creative soul?

What is important to you in your life? Have you fulfilled your dreams? If not, why not?

These are all important questions many of us are asking ourselves after a year and a half of the COVID-19 pandemic. Our lives have been turned upside down. The global world is experiencing a very difficult time of change.

The key to attracting joy and abundance in your life, no matter what is going on in the outside world, is to follow your joy, your happiness.

We all have free will. Choose gratitude and love rather than anger or fear. I have felt the tremendous fear in people as they face this Covid-19 pandemic, which is the opposite of where you need to be to access your intuitive guidance. Avoid going into fear, it is negative and lowers your vibration.

It is important to keep our thoughts and intentions in a high vibration. If you only knew how powerful your thoughts and words are – you would always use positive words. Be a master of your words. Send love and blessings to any negative thought, word or criticism that crosses your mind.

I had been visiting my daughter and family in Texas for several weeks in March 2021. After a year and a half of isolation and restrictions in New England, it felt wonderful to be in the warm 70-degree weather. I was scheduled to return home to Rhode Island, but when I checked the weather forecast for the day of my return flight, it showed freezing weather, a snowstorm and Southwest Airlines had sent an alert that Rhode Island was requesting a 14-day quarantine on returning passengers.

What was I returning to? 14 days alone in cold freezing weather? I suddenly felt a jolt in my body and dread in my heart. I heard my voice say, "You cannot do this!"

I was feeling so conflicted that I decided to sit quietly and meditate for 15 minutes. I asked for guidance on why my body was reacting so strongly against me going home?

Five days later, I am sitting on the patio of my friend's condominium in Marco Island, Florida, listening to the birds sing and watching people walk the white sandy beach. Sounds great? It really happened, all because I trusted my inner guidance and asked for help and my guides delivered me to this sacred retreat. Isn't it lovely how other people, those in the spirit world and those in the physical world, all help us to accomplish a goal?

The first day at the condominium I received a call from my friend Elaine saying, "Hey, we've got a booth!" It was for the upcoming Narragansett Art Festival. We have shared booths in the past for my book signings and her scenic photography. This was wonderful news because all book signings and outside events had been cancelled last year due to COVID.

During a group Zoom meditation that afternoon, a message came through loud and clear. I was strongly guided to the fact that I needed a new book to showcase at the art festival, a book on accessing our intuitive power within. I could see the book cover and flashes of turquoise color across my forehead. Seeing turquoise color in a meditation is a message from Archangel Gabriel. He helps us with communication and with writing and artistic projects.

I shared my experience with the meditation group, and my friend Ruth offered her publishing services and stated, "I am available to work quickly on this project, you must get started writing immediately." In less than a day, I was committed to writing this book!

Isn't it lovely how other people can all work together? Those in the spirit world and those in the physical world all sort of pushed me to get things structured. There is always a role for those who are the colleagues, the compatriots and the fellows that are in your life that will also provide the structures or the little tweaks to put it all together. It is important to participate in a community that shares your creative, artistic or intellectual interests.

So, with all the help from my team, this book will endeavor to teach you some techniques to trust your own intuitive guidance. We are not alone and help is available to us from the spirit world and the physical world. We all know on an inner level what is best for us, we just need to trust it.

The sunset photograph for the cover of the book was taken at the beach on Marco Island while I wrote this book. I think the golden sunset is perfect for the title. I always sense my divine God self in the presence of the sunset and reflect on why I am here and my soul purpose.

Our soul purpose is why we chose to be born on the earth at this very magical, pivotal point in time. My shamanic teacher, Don Oscar Miro-Quesada taught our group over 30 years ago when we first met, that we all agreed 26,000 years ago to come back to the earth and be part of this major historical earth shift. All living beings alive at this time were chosen to be here because of their unique individual gifts. No one else has the knowledge and experience that you do to bring this information to the earth, at this time.

There has been a power struggle between the dark and the light forces in the world for too long. The world desperately needs your light and your individual gifts.

Divine forces are involved in guiding and shaping every person's life whether you are aware of them or not. You are divinely protected by spiritual helpers who are ready to assist. You are not alone. When you are aware and open to them, these spiritual forces can have a very positive impact on your life.

Your intuition is one of the ways these divine forces are able to affect you through these subtle realms. So, if you have not already done so, commit to a practice to develop your intuitive abilities.

I was guided to write this book to teach you some helpful techniques to align your vibration with the higher realms. There are infinite possibilities when you think from a high vibrational state of joy, gratitude and love. Create a life of endless possibilities, your guardian angels, spirit guides, ascended masters, teachers and loved ones in Spirit are all ready to assist you. After this year and a half of aloneness and soul searching, I feel you will find this information very helpful and timely.

Remember the last time you had a magical day?

From the moment you woke up, the entire day floated together so smoothly. The people you met were exactly who you needed to spend time with or they had valuable information for you.

You felt so blessed and may have called it a number 10 day or better yet, a memorable day!

Would you like to have more of these days?

You Can....

Trust It! You have the Power Within You.

****

CHAPTER ONE

Wisdom of Oz

Courage, Curiosity, and a Positive Outlook

We are all incredibly powerful beings, but many do not take control of living their lives, living their soul purpose. Many people feel less than or not worthy of a full and happy life. We can rely on others to give us what we need instead of having the courage to go after it ourselves.

We all remember the famous movie from our childhood, "The Wizard of Oz." It is the most seen film in movie history according to the Library of Congress. It spoke to us on a soul level. We felt the courage, curiosity and positive outlook of all of the characters. They were scared but determined, and all four of them sensed the support and power from their team effect.

It is the perfect metaphor or allegory for life. We watched it over and over again and never grew tired of watching Judy Garland sing "Somewhere over the Rainbow." Rainbows have spiritual and symbolic meaning. A rainbow is a sign of blessing for your ventures, those close to you, and yourself. It is a powerful sign and it can be seen as a message from the Universe or Spirit that you are headed in the right direction.

There are many who felt that the author of the story, L. Frank Baum, wrote the book for the political, economic and social events of America in the 1890's.

I feel the 1939 American musical film produced by Metro-Goldwyn-Mayer and directed by Victor Fleming has so many timely life lessons for all of us during these challenging times of the 21th century. It was nominated for six Academy Awards, including best picture, but lost to "Gone with the Wind," also directed by Fleming.

The overall message is:

> *"Everything you were looking for*
> *was right there with you all along."*

How has one movie had a lasting effect on so many of us, for so many years? It is a classic, like its competition, "Gone with the Wind," the highest-grossing film in history. It too was divinely inspired to help a generation withstand the changes and turmoil of the 1930's and 1940's. Two very difficult decades of turmoil, loss and destruction. It took courage, hope and self-perseverance to survive. We are experiencing a very difficult time in the world, at this time. With the global pandemic of 2020, our lives have been turned upside down. There has been tremendous loss and uncertainty. Fear of the unknown is creating anxiety and PTSD in many young adults and families.

Remember we are not alone in these turbulent times. We have our ancestors' heroic stories of courage to look back on. Remember we are a lot like our grandparents and great grandparents. We have their strength, determination and hope for a better life running through our blood. We can even call on them during meditation and ask for their intuitive guidance on a problem or advise on how to embrace change and face our individual fears.

Taking the time to truly look within and reconnect with who we are and what is our heart's desire? Just like the witch and tornado that Dorothy faced, we too will face challenges and change.

On this journey called life, we're often taught to look *outside* ourselves, we spend time seeking validation, love, happiness and joy from outside sources instead of looking within. ***You have the power within.*** It is located in your heart, but just like the cowardly lion, we don't know it or we don't trust it.

Dorothy represents all of us. She is following the normal road of life seeking happiness and validation externally. She runs away trying to escape her problems. Sounds familiar to many of us but we take our problems with us wherever we go.

Many of us have or will be hit with a tornado and it is the chaos of change. Change isn't easy and can cause us significant upheaval in our lives. It's scary and feels like you don't have control but it is during these times of discomfort that we experience growth and discover who we truly are.

The yellow brick road represents our path to enlightenment. The journey is more important than the destination. You need to experience your journey, face your challenges and fears, in order to learn and recognize the Gift and Power you hold Within Yourself. These are your God given gifts that are needed by the world during these challenging times.

Scarecrow, Tin Man and Cowardly Lion are the companions Dorothy meets along the way.

The scarecrow is searching for a brain. Many times, in life, we stumble around trying to figure things out. We feel confused, have self-doubt and insecurities, and we seek outside ourselves for answers. Intelligence is deeper than knowledge, it is also self-awareness and understanding.

The Tin Man is searching for a heart. We are all looking for love and passion in our lives. We want to feel loved and lead a fulfilling life but we forget to look inside ourselves to discover what is right for us. We have unconditional love and power within our hearts. We come from love, and we will return to love. Love is all there is.

The Cowardly Lion is seeking courage. We too are all seeking the courage to be our authentic selves. It is not easy if we feel and think differently from our parents or peers.

The Wicked Witch represents our fears, which are only an illusion. I'll say it again, Fear is an illusion and will keep appearing in our lives until we stand up and face it. We need to face the fears in our lives that hold us back from becoming our authentic self. Dorothy threw water on the witch and the witch melted away. The water is an analogy to Shining a Light in the Face of Fear to make it disappear. Remember the way to illuminate the darkness is to turn on a light.

Glinda the Good Witch – Glinda is our higher self. Our higher self is always offering us intuitive guidance. We only have to **listen.** Remember when scarecrow asked Glinda why she had not told Dorothy earlier that she had the power all along to go back to Kansas?

Glinda replied, "Because she wouldn't have believed me. She had to learn it for herself."

The Wizard is a fraud, a middle-aged man, with no power. It was all smoke and mirrors. We all encounter a wizard type in our lives, someone or something we think will solve a problem for us. They can be encouraging, but no one can do it for you. The power lies **within you.**

The great Wizard of Oz metaphor is the idea that we think something outside of ourselves has all the answers. We tend to look externally for answers, validation and approval. We forget how powerful we really are. We have the power inside of us all along, we just need to trust and act on it.

****

Free

I Am Free to Reach for The Stars

Today I celebrate my freedom to be exactly who I am.
In all the world, there is no one exactly like me.

My talents, traits, and passions are uniquely my own
and are the tools I need to fulfill my purpose
and reach my potential.

I build on that foundation and I am free to
dream big dreams, make bold plans and
reach for all that life has to offer.

With compassion for myself,
I search my mind to discover whether I have
limited my freedom by believing that I may not
have what it takes to live the life of my dreams.

I shift my focus from the matters of the outer world
and align myself with the spiritual world,
the world of pure freedom.

I am grateful for my freedom and
for the gifts of life, hope and dreams.

Printed with permission of Unity, publisher of Daily Word (R) magazine.

CHAPTER TWO

Intuition

Choose to Cultivate Your Spiritual Guidance

You are a spiritual being having a physical experience, not a physical being having a spiritual experience. You are a divine being of light!

You have a human and a non-human side to you. Your human side resides in your mind; your non-human side is your soul, it resides in the higher realms, you access it through your heart. Don't just identify with your human experience.

You are not your mind. The mind is necessary, but it is not who you are. It overrides your wisdom and the internal guidance of your soul. It is time to take back your power by accessing the intuitive guidance of your soul.

The mind constantly reminds us that we are not enough. We are too thin, too heavy, too short, too tall, or we need more education, more money, more toys to fit in with "The Jones's."

If you listen to your mind, it assures confusion and it will keep your heart closed. We need an open heart to access intuitive guidance, unconditional love and peace. An open heart also raises our vibration and provides access to intuitive wisdom and knowledge.

Most of your stress comes from the way you respond to a situation, not the way life is. Try to adjust your attitude. Change how you see things. Look for the good in all situations. Take the lesson and find new opportunities to grow. Let all the extra stress, worrying and overthinking go.

There are no accidents, everything is in divine order. You may not be able to see or understand it in this present moment but at some point, you may be able to look back at this time and see the lesson or the silver lining in the situation. Some of our greatest helpers and lifetime friends come into our lives during our most difficult times.

A loving being is who you really are. Try to accept everyone just the way they are. Accept your feelings and give compassion to yourself and others. This will free you from the emotions and enable you to listen to your inner guidance, the Source of your true inner peace. Your heart is open when you are at peace.

Be in gratitude and say thank you, thank you for all the beauty, the love, and the harmony that is in your life.

Surround yourself with the beauty in nature. It is available daily and absolutely free!

A great way to start your day is to get up early and behold the beauty in the sunrise. A daily walk in your neighborhood, on a bike path, the beach or in the woods is perfect for nurturing your soul, releasing stressful energy, and allowing your creative instincts to flourish.

We are all creative beings and we are most happy and productive when we are in alignment with our natural state. We were meant to be happy, joyful and loving! I'm sure you have all experienced these feeling when you are doing something you love and enjoy. More time should be spent in this creative process.

Unfortunately, we are all taught at an early age to shut down our inner voice and conform. Many were conditioned to block out their inner guidance and to just go along with the status quo.

Over time our inner voice grows dimmer until we have a major crisis in our life or life changing event. Then we realize the tools we gathered from childhood no longer work for us.

Intuitive Guidance is the key to accepting your true gifts in life. When you ask your soul to guide you, you are acknowledging you are not alone in this world. You can receive intuitive guidance from many sources. The most common ones are God, your higher self, Archangels, guardian angels, spirit guides, deceased family members, ascended masters and teachers.

Intuitive guidance is always present. We can access it 24/7 if we are in the right frequency and state of mind. There are different frequencies existing on earth at the same time. Our thoughts, words and actions determine our frequency.

It is easier to access intuitive guidance when we are in a high vibration of gratitude, appreciation and love. Our vibration is lower when we are fearful, angry or negative. Being in a low vibration will cause interference and static when you try to access intuitive guidance. Like an old fashion radio with a tuning dial, you had to fine tune the dial to get the station at the right frequency to come in clearly.

The same is true of accessing the higher intuitive realms. The reason we can't hear it sometimes is because our minds are full of fearful, negative thoughts or how we think things *should* be. We need to spend some time each day in quiet meditation and listen to our inner voice.

The soul uses a variety of methods for communicating with us, but the most direct route is the way of intuition. It is not a verbal language, but a language of feelings. The ability to listen and trust your intuition enables you to move with ease and freedom in the world and protect yourself from unnecessary pain or harm.

For example, if you are dating someone and there is an uneasy feeling about him/her, your intuition is speaking up. If you choose to ignore it, then you are responsible for the consequences that might come about. When intuition is ignored or bypassed, a deep sense of anxiety sets in. Whenever the element of frustration enters any area of your life -- you are not listening to the wisdom of your intuition. The way to eliminate the frustration is by getting quiet to clear the mind, so it becomes empty and ready to receive the guidance.

Take a few moments to be in a receptive mode. Close your eyes, take some deep cleansing breaths and bring your awareness into the center of your heart. In this calm space, tune into your intuition and ask for guidance. Ask yourself a yes or no question about the situation and see how you feel in your heart. If you feel anxious or uneasy, it is a no reply. If you feel relaxed and peaceful, it is a yes reply. Trust the guidance that you are receiving.

What is this guidance? It is actually the universe guiding you via your intuition. It is constantly guiding you whether you are conscious of it or not.

When you begin to operate from the realm of intuition, you automatically move to the next level in your development – self-authority.

Because the language of the universe is not literal, your cultivation and understanding of how the universe speaks to you and guides you is crucial. By remaining receptive, being aware of the signs, signals and messages of Guidance, your life will take on a completely new dimension and meaning.

For example, you've been thinking about moving from your apartment and wondered if you could afford to buy instead of renting. You were running late for work, but decided to stop at the coffee shop to pick up the local real estate magazine. As you wait for your order, you begin talking with the woman next to you who notices the magazine and mentions she is a realtor and just listed the most amazing property for a first-time home buyer; no money down, and the seller is offering to pay all closing costs.

Coincidence? Not at all. You followed your natural impulse and ended up being in the right place at the right time, in order to meet the person who could help take you to the next level. You could have resisted the urge to pick up the coffee because you were running late, but instead, you were mindful and therefore benefited greatly.

Besides your intuition, things you read, see or hear throughout your day that capture your attention are also clues of how this Guidance manifests or tries to impart information to you about your life. You may receive a message from a song, reading an article, or receiving a phone call; having a strange encounter or a chance meeting with someone from the past, or receiving a message in a dream.

When we say yes to the river of life, we become attuned to the flow and source of all life. You know that life has a plan for you. Pay attention to what is coming out of the flow now. Every choice in every moment has an effect and can potentially affect your destiny. You can affect the experience you are having by managing your thoughts and attitude. An attitude of appreciation, gratitude and positive words and thoughts tunes you to the positive flow of energy.

The rest, you just surrender it to source, to the divine. You go with the flow of the river. Your desire to control falls away when you surrender and trust that all is in divine and perfect order, as it was meant to be. Trust allows life to carry you where it will. You will know when you are fulfilling your destiny by how you feel in your heart. Your heart will feel naturally happy and ready to move forward with your new life.

The key is to listen to your heart and trust your gut feelings. What you feel in your heart or a gut feeling is your body receiving an intuitive message and your body is responding to the emotion. We are all getting gentle reminders or confirmations from spirit all the time. I call these gentle reminders, confirmations, signs or synchronicities.

Can you think of some gentle reminders or synchronicities you may have received but discounted them as an odd co-incidence? Trust me, they are not! The more you acknowledge them, the more help you will receive.

Once you get in the flow, you will trust your intuition more and be receptive to the signs. You will feel more comfortable and secure in the world. You will feel like you belong here and that somehow, despite everything that has gone wrong in your life, it was all a learning experience, and things will work out in your best interest in the end. Divine Guidance will make sure of it.

****

CHAPTER THREE

Meditation

Mindfulness

Meditation is a practice where an individual uses a technique such as mindfulness, which focuses the mind on a particular object, thought, or activity. This focusing will cause your mind to relax, slow your attention, and heighten your awareness to achieve an emotionally calm state.

There are endless benefits of meditation. One of them is that you're able to focus and direct your consciousness, which is precisely what we need while tapping into our inner guidance. The emotional benefits of meditation can include:

1. Gaining a new perspective on stressful situations
2. Building skills to manage your stress
3. Increasing self-awareness
4. Focusing on the present
5. Reducing negative emotions
6. Increasing imagination and creativity
7. Increasing patience and tolerance

In a mindfulness practice, we are learning how to return to, and remain in the present moment so that we can anchor ourselves in the here and now without judgment.

A daily meditation practice helps you receive intuitive guidance and inspiration from your higher self and your spiritual team. Intuitive guidance is always present but, we have to be a vibrational match and in the right state of mind to receive it.

We can't hear it when our minds are full of thoughts and our own ideas of how things should be.

The best and easiest way is to start a daily meditation practice. We "practice" mindfulness so we can learn how to recognize when our minds are doing their normal everyday acrobatics, and maybe take a pause from that for just a little while, so we can choose what we'd like to focus on.

How to Meditate

Meditation is simpler than most people think. It gets easier and more relaxing the more you practice it. There is no right or wrong way. It is a practice of stilling our active minds and getting in touch with our hearts. It is our natural state. Your body and mind will thank you for starting a daily practice.

It is always important for you to set your intention or ask for help before you start your daily meditation. Write it down on a piece of paper or keep a journal, to make it more concrete. Your focused intention can be a phrase or single word.

Make sure you're somewhere where you can relax into this process, set a timer for 5-10 minutes. You can gradually increase the time up to 15 – 30 minutes as you progress. Set your intention to create sacred space and ask for divine protection and clarity. Only beings of Light, Love and Compassion are allowed in your sacred space. Place your hands on your lap or in prayer position. Just make sure you are comfortable. You may want a blanket nearby.

1. Sit comfortably with your feet on the ground.

2. Be as still as a statue and then say, "I put a baby smile on my lips."

3. Close your eyes and become aware of your breath. Inhale and exhale through your nose with your mouth closed. As you inhale, raise your tongue to the roof of your mouth, hold to a count of three, then drop your tongue to the bottom of your mouth.

Concentrate your focus on your inhalation and exhalation. Follow the sensation of your breath, as it goes in and out. Now gently allow your awareness to drop to your heart. Let each inhalation fill your heart with golden healing light and each exhalation release any stress, tension or worry.

4. Notice when your mind wanders. Inevitably, your attention will leave the breath and wander to other places – simply return your attention to the breath and your heart.

5. Be kind to your wandering mind. Don't judge yourself or obsess over the content of the thoughts you find yourself lost in. Just let them pass and come back to your breath.

6. Focus on your breath and become aware of everything you feel, sense, see and hear.

7. You may feel a sense of warmth or flushing, chills down your back or arms, uneasy feeling in your gut, flashes of light, sensation of coldness in one area of your body, splashes of vibrant color across your forehead and eyes. Some people feel so relaxed they appear to be asleep but they can still hear sounds in the room.

8. When the timer chimes. Take a few moments to gently open your eyes. Take a moment and notice any sounds in the environment and how your body feels right now, you should feel more relaxed and calmer.

9. Keep a pad and pen near-by so you can make a few notes about what came up for you in the meditation. Did you ask for guidance, if so, make note of your any

thoughts and or emotions that came up for you. Draw a picture of what you saw if you had a lot of visual images.

A quiet mind and body will allow your intuitive guidance the opportunity to speak to you. Keep track of the guidance you receive during your meditation. The information usually will expand in more detail in future meditations.

You can ask for guidance or prayers for other people, situations or upcoming events. Know that your prayers will be heard and assistance will be on the way.

There are endless benefits of meditation. One of them is that you're able to focus and direct your consciousness, which is precisely what you need to do to tap into your inner guidance

Allow yourself to be completely open to the limitless possibilities. Once you ask, have complete confidence that it will be given. Ask and you shall receive!

Don't second guess yourself. Set the intention and wait for the answer to be revealed to you. It may come in many ways. You may receive guidance during your meditation in words or symbols. You may receive the information in a phone call, text or an odd coincidence or chance meeting. Be open to receiving guidance within a two-week period.

Phases of the Moon

It is also beneficial to utilize the phases of the moon each month for manifesting. The New Moon is new beginnings. It is the best time to ask for guidance and spiritual helpers for a project or a new idea. You will usually see the results within the week leading up to the Full Moon. The Full Moon brings manifestation. I always plan the undaunting task of completing my tax return during the full moon weekend leading up to the tax due date. It really helps to complete the task in a focused manner.

****

CHAPTER FOUR

Seven Chakras

Energy Points in the Body

Your inner guidance always translates the messages for you in the best way you can understand. It may use familiar sensations, colors, emotions or feelings.

If you are empathetic, you may feel a sensation or pain in different parts of your body. The organ or area of the sensation may correspond to one of the 7 chakras in the body and the emotional charge associated with each one.

Chakra means "wheel" and refers to energy points in your body. They are thought to be spinning discs of energy that should stay "open" and aligned, as they correspond to bundles of nerves, major organs and areas of our energetic body, which affect our emotional and physical well-being.

Each of these seven main chakras has a corresponding number, name, color and specific area of the spine from the sacrum to the crown of the head.

1st Root Chakra: at the base of your spine, in the tailbone area. The color is Red and represents our physical identity, stability, security, and feeling grounded both physically and emotionally.

2nd Sacral Chakra: just below the bellybutton. The color is Orange and represents our feelings of self-worth, specifically our self-worth around pleasure, sexuality and creativity.

3rd Solar Plexus Chakra: in the upper abdomen, in the stomach area. The color is Yellow and represents our self-esteem and confidence. It's the chakra of our personal power.

4th Heart Chakra: in the center of the chest, just above the heart. The color is Green and its meaning is Love and compassion.

People with heart chakra blocks often put others first, to their own detriment. It's the middle of the seven chakras, so it bridges the gap between our upper and lower chakras, and it also represents our ability to love and connect to others. When out of alignment, it can make us feel lonely, insecure, and isolated.

5th Throat Chakra: located in the throat. It is the color Blue and represents communication. As one would expect, this chakra is connected to our ability to communicate verbally.

Blocks or misalignments can be seen when people are dominating conversations, gossiping, or speaking without thinking. It can also be having trouble speaking your mind or not being allowed to speak.

When in alignment, you will speak and listen with compassion and feel confident when you speak because you know you are being true to yourself with your words.

6th Third Eye Chakra: located between the eyes, on the forehead. The color is Indigo and its meaning is Intuition and Imagination. People who have trouble listening to reality or who are not in touch with their intuition may have a block. When open and in alignment, people will follow their intuition and be able to see the big picture.

7th The Crown Chakra: located at the top of the head. Its color is Violet or White and represents awareness and intelligence. It is linked to every other chakra (and therefore every organ in this system), and so it affects not just all of those organs, but also our brain and nervous system.

It is considered the chakra of enlightenment and represents our connection to spirituality and our higher self. Those with a blocked crown chakra may seem narrow-minded, skeptical, or stubborn. When this chakra is open, it is thought to help keep all the other chakras open and to bring the person bliss and enlightenment.

As these are all energetic centers of the body that correspond to feelings, one of them probably resonated with you as you were reading. A different one may resonate with you tomorrow.

It's likely that one resonates with you more than any others as a continuous problem. These chakras are sources of information and healing for us and we will feel sensation and pain more often when emotions are coming up for healing.

The knowledge of the chakras and their corresponding colors and meaning will be so helpful as you interpret the sensations you feel in your body during meditation.

As an example, if you sit on the floor to meditate, after several minutes of sitting still, you may experience discomfort in your hips or legs. Acknowledge the discomfort, focus your intention to send healing light to the area with each exhale of your breath. Slowly the discomfort will start to disappear. Since the pain was in your first chakra, ask if there is a message for you from this release. The hard floor may not have been the cause of your discomfort.

Because the First Root Chakra represents our physical identity, stability, feeling grounded and secure (both physically and emotionally), be open in your meditation for guidance to identify and heal this area of your life.

If you feel pressure in your throat or start to cough during meditation, this can be an indication from your Fifth Throat Chakra (located in your throat and represents communication). This chakra is connected to your ability to communicate verbally. Having trouble speaking your mind or not being allowed to speak is not healthy for you. Send healing energy to your throat to release and heal this imbalance.

Many of our prayer requests and intuitive questions may stem from blockages or issues relating to these chakras, so it is important to learn and study these chakras in more depth.

An acupuncturist is extremely helpful to work on balancing and healing your chakra issues.

****

CHAPTER FIVE

Whole-Body Movement

Dowsing Technique

Dowsers use a pendulum or dowsing rods to read the flow of energy in the earth. We have a positive and negative energy flow constantly running through our bodies. Our bodies are giant dowsing rods.

We can use our bodies as personal dowsing rods to receive a positive or negative response to a question. You can access this energy through Whole Body Movement or the Intuitive Hand dowsing methods.

Use one or both of these two simple methods whenever you have a question that can be answered with a straight yes or no response.

Exercise to Determine Your Personal Body Response to a YES Question.

Take a moment to surround yourself with a white golden light of divine protection, starting at the top of your head and encircling your body to the bottom of your feet. This creates a sacred bubble of protection and connects you to higher guidance. Ask your guides to protect and guide you during your dowsing session.

Stand upright with both feet firmly planted on the ground. Center yourself and raise your head up from your shoulders. Imagine yourself as a very strong, tall tree.

Close your eyes and state your intention to access your whole-body movement dowsing method. Ask to be shown how your body will respond to a Yes and a No answer. (the most common response is a forward or backward movement of your body but some may go side to side)

Take 3 deep breaths, center yourself and say, "My name is _____ " 3 times. (use your full name or nickname if you have always been known by it)

Notice how your body moves.

Did it move forward?

Did it move Backwards?

Whatever direction your body moved is your YES response. Say thank you and make note of this response.

Now we will determine your body movement to a No response.

Exercise to Determine Your Personal Body Response to a NO Question.

Stand upright again with both feet firmly planted on the ground. Center yourself and raise your head up from your shoulders. Imagine yourself as a very strong, tall tree.

Take 3 deep breaths again, center yourself and say an incorrect name such as:

"My name is _____," (Donald Duck, Micky Mouse, or Harry Potter). Say one of these names 3 times and notice your body response.

Make note of the direction your body moved to this incorrect or No answer. This will be your No response to your personal dowsing questions. Say thank you and make note of this response.

Isn't it amazing to feel the pull within your body to a correct and incorrect answer! This is an invaluable tool you can use at any time to access your intuitive guidance.

Always Ask for Permission before Starting

Now that you know your body's response to a yes/no question, it is always important to ask if you have permission before you start to ask the questions. You do this by asking three simply questions before you start the dowsing process.

1. Do I have permission to ask a question?

2. Is it the right time for me to ask?

3. Am I the right person to ask this question?

If you receive a NO to any of these questions, respect it and wait to ask the question at another time. Maybe in the next day or two. Always honor what you receive. Dowsing should only be used when there is a "need to know."

Remember you cannot ask personal or private questions for someone else without seeking their personal permission first. We cannot interfere in someone else's life without their permission. Technically, we should always ask if we have permission before speaking on someone's behalf.

Keeping a Journal

It's best to keep a journal when you first start dowsing. Make note of the date and write out your questions, then record the yes or no answer you receive.

1. Make your question very specific.

2. The correct framing of the question can only have a yes or no answer.

3. Only ask one question at a time.

4. Never more than 3 questions in one session.

Many people are naturally sensitive and simple training and practice can turn this ability into a very powerful personal tool. You may encounter an answer that does not make sense to you immediately. Don't worry, within a short time period, you will have more information. This is why it is good to write the information down in your journal.

****

CHAPTER SIX

Intuitive Hand Method

Dowsing Technique

Another way to access intuitive guidance through body dowsing is to use your hands. You are accessing the positive and negative energy flow running through your hands and fingers. You can do this exercise in a sitting position.

A YES Response

Take a moment to surround yourself with a white golden light of divine protection, starting at the top of your head and encircling your body to the bottom of your feet. This creates a sacred bubble of protection and connects you to higher guidance. Ask your guides to protect and guide you during your dowsing session.

Make a circle with your thumb and forefinger on your non-dominant hand. Take your dominant hand and enclose your thumb and forefinger inside this circle.

Center yourself and take a deep breath and set your intention to be shown a yes answer to a question.

You are asking yourself the same name questions as in the first exercise.

Take 3 deep breaths, center yourself and say, "My name is _____" 3 times. (use your full name or nickname if you have always been known by it)

Watch how your fingers responded. Did the circle with your non-dominant hand stay strong and closed? This will be a "yes" response.

Example: YES

A NO Response

Make a circle with your thumb and forefinger on your non-dominant hand. Take you dominant hand and enclose your thumb and forefinger inside this circle.

Take a few deep breaths to center yourself and set your intention to be shown a No answer.

Say, "My name is_____ Donald Duck," Micky Mouse, or Harry Potter. Say one of these names 3 times and notice your body response.

Did your fingers in the circle of your non-dominant hand let go and allow your dominant-hand's circle to pull it apart?

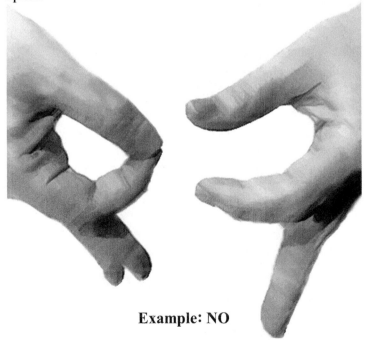

Example: NO

Isn't that amazing, how the flow of energy relaxes to a no answer and stays strong for a yes answer?

This will be your universal key to asking a quick question.

These are extremely valuable exercises to help you focus your intentions and not waste time on unnecessary endeavors. I notice many women using this method when trying to decide if they should purchase an item at a clothing store.

****

CHAPTER SEVEN

Thoughts are Things

You are here for a reason and that reason is discovered by following your heart and listening to your intuition.

What makes you feel joyful and creative? If you are older now, think back to your childhood. What did you love to play or do when you were ages nine to eleven years old?

There is a wonderful book called, *What Color is Your Parachute?* by Richard N. Bolles that helps people make career and job decisions based on what made you happiest when you were still a child, ages nine to eleven. His research showed adults who were the most happy and successful in their careers were working at what they loved to play as a child. That's pretty amazing.

I believe we are also most in alignment with our Soul Purpose with this career choice. So, connect in with this little girl or boy during your meditation time. Ask your higher self and spirit guides to bring back the important memories and feelings from that time in your life.

What were some of your magical moments? Write them down and think of how you can apply them to your life today. Never discount children's play. We are in our most joyful state of mind, when we are playing and laughing.

You were following your intuition when you were young and it is not too late to listen to it again. We do this when we meditate. Give yourself the luxury of being a kid again. You have been a grown up long enough.

Everything around you are energy and energy vibrates and moves at different rates of speed. Just because you don't see it, that doesn't mean it doesn't exist. All living things in nature are energy and they vibrate and give off energy. We can feel the positive energy of nature when we are by the ocean or walking by a flower garden or trees. Animals also have a strong energy field and we can feel their love and affection. We are all receiving and giving out our individual energy frequency.

We are also influenced by the collective energy consciousness. Positive, creative, and joyful people reside at a higher frequency and sad, angry or depressed people resides at a lower frequency and this can be felt and absorbed by those around them.

Like attracts like. I'm sure you have noticed this with some of your family or friends. We are more receptive to receive signs and synchronicities when we have a positive upbeat, glass is ½ full attitude. It brightens our day and everyone else's.

We have to be conscious of our energy field and know when it needs protection. Notice when you feel happy and joyful around some people, while with others, you feel totally drained after being with them.

You are not imagining these vibrational shifts. They are very real and over time, they can drain you of your energy. There are only two types of vibrations, positive and negative, and they are being broadcast by feelings.

Thoughts are things. A famous quote by Henry Ford comes to mind on this subject.

*"Whether you think you can or think you can't,
you're right."*

Every thought emits a frequency to the universe, and this frequency goes back to the origin. Think about that! When we have a negative thought – anger, fear or gossip – all this comes back to you. The same is true of the positive, so it is important that you set a conscious intent to speak well of others and send them good will.

The people you spend time with either personally, at work or on social media directly influence your vibrational frequency. If you surround yourself with happy, positive people, you will raise your vibration to match theirs. Learn how to cultivate more positive thoughts and refuse to engage in gossip or negative conversations.

Being with a negative person will actually lower your vibration and drain your energy. You may have a family member or co-worker that drains your energy unknowingly.

Your sense of peace and well-being is totally dependent upon their well-being. This a real problem for many empaths who feel they can help or save this person, but it all goes back to free will.

You are actually disempowering them, not helping them. It is more beneficial to teach them how to access their own intuitive power by becoming aware and shifting their negative thoughts and feelings to positive and creative thoughts and ideas. Maybe ask them the question. "What did you love to play or do when you were ages nine to eleven years old?" Maybe make a play date with them to help them remember their childhood joy and happiness. Encourage them to do more of this or take classes. You may even want to join them.

Do not allow them to beat you up verbally, energetically, or psychologically. If they are mean and threatening, disengage from the conversation. Walk away or hang up the phone. Continue to do this until they are ready to talk in a civil manner.

It can be hard to do to a family member but it does work. Set your intentions for what you wish to accomplish and accept nothing less. You are doing them a favor; this is a lesson they should have learned a long time ago. They will thank you one day when they are happy again.

Music is very powerful. It is not only the words but the vibration of the musical notes. Pay attention to the lyrics of the music. Is it an upbeat positive song of joy and encouragement or a song of sadness, betrayal or abandonment, all this will interfere with what you are feeling and trying to manifest. Remember your vibration aligns with what you feel in your life.

Television, movies and videos have an influence on your vibrational energy. When you look at programs that deal with death, betrayal and misfortune, your brain accepts this as reality and releases a whole chemistry into your body, which affects your vibrational frequency. Notice how you feel after watching a violent movie or television show. Do you ever have trouble falling asleep after watching these programs? If you do, meditate and cleanse your energy field of these negative feelings and emotions before bed.

Your home or office environment affects your vibrational frequency. Clean up the clutter, organize and clean your space and request that others do the same. Feng Shui is a wonderful ancient Chinese modality of placement that uses energy forces to harmonize individuals with their surrounding environment in an auspicious manner. It is over 3,500 years old and works with how the Chi, or energy, circulates inside a home or work environment.

There are many auspicious color and furniture placement remedies suggestions to increase the energy flow to benefit your family or business.

Think before you speak, words can hurt. Don't mix bad words with your bad mood. You will have many opportunities to change your mood, but you will never get the opportunity to replace the words you spoke. To keep your frequency high, it is essential to eliminate negative thoughts. This includes complaining and getting involved in gossip and drama.

Being in a state of gratitude positively affects your vibration. Especially during this stressful year, it's important to reflect on all of the blessings you have. Being grateful for all the blessings in your life reminds you what a gift the present moment is for everyone. Remember today is a gift, that is why it is called the present and tomorrow is promised to no one.

****

CHAPTER EIGHT

Signs
and
Synchronicities

"Ask & You Shall Receive"

I wrote my first book, *Believe In Forever: How to Recognize Signs from Departed Loved Ones* to help the newly grieved be open to receive signs from their loved ones.

We let go of the physical body when we die and our soul goes home to a higher vibration than the human eye can see. When you quiet the mind in meditation or say prayers for them, you raise your vibration. Sensing this, your loved ones will lower their vibration, creating a meeting space in the middle for you to receive a message from them.

Our departed loved ones, guardian angels, and spiritual guides are always available and they send us intuitive messages through signs and synchronicities. These signs will have a significant meaning for us.

Our loved ones are near shortly after passing to help us with our grief, and to let us know their love for us is eternal. They also come to celebrate joyful occasions. Family weddings, holidays, graduations, funerals and the birth of new children. After speaking with grieving families, I realized many people were unaware of what the signs were and I felt they were missing out on this wonderful experience my family had shared for so many years.

These are the 12 Most Common Signs:

- Dream visitations
- Sensing their presence – chills or goose bumps
- Feeling their touch
- Smelling their fragrance (common also with pets)
- Hearing their voice in your head
- Unexpected electrical activity – lights blink
- Finding coins
- Finding feathers
- Synchronistic messages, signs or coincidences.
- Movement of objects – missing keys, painting falls off wall.
- Birds – Hawks are male, father presence.
  Red cardinals are female, mother, grandmother presence.
- Seeing an apparition (cloud of smoke, hologram, orbs in pictures.
- Unknown phone calls

Dream Visitation

Dreams are the most common way to be visited by those in Spirit and to access intuitive guidance. It is when we are most relaxed and are naturally connecting with intuitive guidance.

These dreams can start as early as the first few days after a loved one's passing and continue sporadically for years. They may appear to you in a beautiful place, a park, or garden doing something they loved to do. Some are playing bridge, golf, fishing or just sitting on a bench.

There will be other people at the event and you may notice them in the distance. They will suddenly notice you and get very excited, as they draw closer. They usually are surrounded by a golden hue of light and look radiant. They are smiling, happy and appear younger. They will be able to speak, walk or dance again, even if they were incapacitated before they died.

They may give you a message. "I love you." "I can walk again," "I am happy." They may tell you all the exciting things they have been doing. I have heard of people wanting to stay with their loved ones during these visits and being told, "It is not your time; I am still here for you, and I will be there to greet you when it is your time."

Your deceased family member may appear to you with other deceased family members showing you, they are not alone, they have all connected on the other side - even with the family pet.

My daughter, Bethany, went to a psychic medium with a request to her father that for her to truly believe it was him, he had to show up with something only she would recognize.

As the medium mentioned she felt Rick's presence, she mentioned he was pulling a red wagon. As he drew closer to her, she noticed there was a small black animal in the wagon leaning over the side. It did not make much sense to the medium, but Bethany knew exactly what he was showing her. The black animal was Blackie, her pet guinea pig who loved to eat all the vegetables from her father's garden. He would lean over the side of his cage squealing when he heard Rick come home from work. Bethany had a red wagon and it was used in the garden. It was a clear message that only Bethany would understand.

It was very important to Rick that Bethany believe it was him because he cautioned her about her boyfriend, he did not like him or trust him. He warned her to stop seeing him. Bethany really liked this young man and could not possibly understand why her father would say she should stop seeing him.

She had a recording of the session and we both listened again, there was no mistake. Rick clearly sensed danger and told her. "You must stop dating him." What do you do with this type of information? It only took about a week before a rumor started to surface that truth and honesty were not high on this young man's virtue list. No matter how much he denied the information, Bethany trusted and followed her father's guidance and ended the relationship.

This information was not available to anyone at the time of the reading. The medium was not from our city so she could not have possibly known this information. It showed us how Rick was able to see ahead and was trying to protect her from future heartache. A father's love and protection of his children is eternal. They will always be watching out for you. Pay attention for reassuring signs or synchronicities from them.

Everyone is Available to You in the Spirit Realm

My husband came to me in a dream one night so excited! He told me he was able to sit and talk with all the people he had admired during his life time. All he had to do was think of them and they would magically appear on a bench next to him to have a one-on-one conversation, and he got to ask them all the questions he had pondered during his life. How amazing is that!

You wake up from these dreams with a very vivid memory and recollection that does not fade. You remember these visitations and hold them deep in your heart. As time go on, your loved ones may give you helpful advice on important life decisions, should you sell the house, move on to a new relationship, or deliver messages of hope and love.

Many people claim they don't dream or can't remember their dreams. For this reason, I devised a method for remembering all the important points of my dreams:

1. Keep a pencil and pad beside your by bed. When you wake up from a dream, do not turn on the light, immediately write down the key points on the paper and try to go back into the dream state.

2. In the morning, before you move a muscle, take the piece of paper and read what you wrote and add more content.

3. Stop and think of the feeling and emotions of the dream message.

It is so important to do these three steps because we lose 70% of our memory of the dream within seconds of stepping out of bed. We retain the emotions but not the facts. The facts help us understand the emotional component of the dream.

Sensing Their Presence

Sensing a presence can be a little scary for some people. They don't mean to alarm you. Only their physical body is gone, not their vibrational essence.

You were able to recognize them when they entered a room before and nothing has changed. Your energy field will remain open to their loving presence forever. You may notice a shift in energy when they are around, you may experience chills down your back or the hair stands up on your arm, as you were speaking about them, while asking them for advice.

You may sense a supporting hand on your shoulder or a feather like feel on your cheek. (I personally think this is a gentle kiss.) You might feel like someone is sitting next to you in the evenings while you read a book or watch their favorite sports team or television show.

Feeling Their Touch

A hug, a brush on your hair, a sense someone is holding your hand or your shoulder, a gentle touch on your back. These are some of the most comforting forms of connections that can happen. I have felt a gentle push or nudge forward sometimes when I hesitate, I take this as an indication to move forward on a decision. It is always a good choice.

Feeling your loved one's touch is most common to sense in the days following their passing. They come to check on their loved ones and try to comfort them in their grief. They can feel your pain and sadness.

We are still so connected to each other, and we are actually receiving their love and support. They are trying to show us that they are not far and they can still hear us.

Smelling Their Fragrance

Smells from Spirit often come through immediately after someone we love has passed. The ability to smell the fragrance from a deceased loved one is called clairalience.

It is very much connected with our memory. Like any other intuitive sense, you can get specific information about your loved one in Spirit through clairalience. You may smell their perfume or another smell associated with them. For example, cigarette smoke, chocolate chip cookies, flowers, or spices.

In addition to smelling smoke, seeing a puff of smoke near family photographs is a clear indication a loved one in Spirit is present. Take a moment and think of the month and day. Is today a birthday or anniversary for you or your family members displayed in the photographs. You may get chills when you say the correct name. Acknowledge their presence and sit quietly to receive their love.

These smells will come out of the blue and be very strong. In fact, you may ask or look to see who has entered the room, only to discover you are still totally alone.

I had the most fragrant smell of red roses in my office on the first Valentine's Day after Rick's passing. It was so strong; I was sure a colleague of mine had put them on my desk. As I walked into my office, I discovered I was mistaken, no roses!

I knew immediately it was Rick and thanked him for this beautiful gift. The smell continued and slightly dimmed over a 5-day period, about the normal time the fragrance would last from physical flowers.

This happened again another time after my good friend, Lorrie helped me move my younger daughter into her college dorm room. The smell of roses was so strong in the back seat of the car, Lorrie continued to look in the back seat thinking we had left something in the car of my daughter's belongings.

Hearing Their Voice

This is called clairaudience. It is possible to hear a voice externally, as though someone is speaking to you in human form but this is rare unless you have clairaudient abilities. It is more common to hear a voice internally, through thought or word transference. The hearing appears inside your head.

A common phrase or expression may pop into your mind. You may hear your loved one call your name. Do you talk to your husband, grandmother, or best friend in Spirit, while you are doing something they enjoyed?

Do you wait for them to answer? You should. What relative doesn't love to chat with you and get caught up on your life. The answer can come very quickly.

They are in a higher vibration in spirit so sometimes they may answer you before you finish speaking the words. Be open to receiving a *yes* confirmation.

If you don't hear a loved one's voice, you may notice a temporary ringing or buzzing in your ear when they are present or receive a chill down your back.

Electrical Activity

We are all energy and energy runs through all things, especially electrical devices. Many of those in Spirit learn early on that they can move and manipulate electrical devices to get our attention. Sometimes it is unintentional, their excitement can cause electrical devices to beep, blink or turn on.

Smoke alarms are very sensitive, my father started a tradition of setting off the smoke detectors with three short beeps for three nights in a row starting with the night of his funeral.

After my brother's funeral, we were not alarmed, actually pleasantly surprised when the alarms beeped three times for three nights. It was an added consolation that my brother was with my father.

The lights can dim or flicker when you mention their name on holidays. Children's toys can suddenly talk or an old clock can start to chime, even though it has not been wound or batteries changed in years!

Please don't be alarmed or think you are crazy! You are not. Take a moment and thank them for coming and tell them how you are doing or what is new. They are visiting just like they always did, sending you their love and support.

Phone Calls

Many people discount this as an odd coincidence but pay attention if it happens shortly after a loved one passes.

The phone will ring, sometimes in the middle of the night but it can occur, at any time of day. It may have an unknown number or it may be their phone number. You pick it up and just heard static on the other line. It lasts for a long time and you may hear distance sounds or partial words.

They are trying to speak a word or two, but mostly it is a message they are near you. Don't hang up,

I have found the static can get clearer overtime.

The phone is an electrical object that can be affected by their energy entering the room. This usually happens within the first few months.

Songs on the Radio

The radio can turn on all by itself and play one song that has a great significance to you. A television show or movie may appear that has a special meaning or message for you. Be open to these synchronicities.

My husband Rick's favorite song was "My Heart Will Go On" from the movie Titanic. It became his personal calling card to let me know he was with me. The lyrics had significant meaning to both of us. I feel this song by James Horner beautifully describes the eternal bond of love we hold in our hearts for someone we love.

Celine Dion sings this song beautifully and has a YouTube link with the lyrics superimposed that I think you will enjoy reading. This is a great song to listen to before a meditation to access intuitive guidance from a loved one.

A personal example for me was my clock radio beside my bed turning on at 3:30 a.m. playing the Titanic song, "My Heart Will Go On" and then turning off all by itself! At first it freaked me out, but it usually happened when I was worried or overthinking a project at work or something about our daughters. I was happy to have my husband's guidance and support.

Finding Coins

Coins are a very popular sign. Many people report finding a penny, dime or quarter in very unusual places immediately after a loved one passes. They are usually in an odd location or you get an intuitive hit to look down and there it is.

Fathers and grandparents are famous for leaving coins on the doorstep, as you enter or leave your house.

My friend Sara told me a funny story of her deceased husband Gregg. He would leave her pennies all the time when she went out. After a while, she jokingly suggested he up the ante and asked him to leave her dimes instead. All of a sudden, she started noticing dimes instead of the usual pennies.

She thought this was fun and asked him to up the ante again. She was in a store parking lot and noticed a dollar bill rolling along on the ground. She picked it up and held it in her hand thinking she would overhear someone in the store, who had dropped it out of their pocket, but she did not.

After returning to her car, she took a moment to unroll the bill and to her surprise, it was a $100.00 bill. She felt it was Gregg and he had really upped the ante. I don't know about you, but I like how she used a positive affirmation in a fun way and her request was honored abundantly.

A Synchronistic Message,
Sign, or Coincidence

Accessing your intuitive guidance can come during the course of your normal day, whether you are at work, home with your family or spending time in nature. It is actually easier for you to notice and receive messages when you are less distracted and out in nature. When you ASK for a tangible sign, you are likely to receive it.

This is a new realm for many people and a huge learning curve, but once you are open to this perspective and work with it, you will never forget it. Spirit has a good sense of humor.

Once you receive a single sign, time and time again, you will start to trust your own intuition. Keep your eyes open for other signs and synchronicities and explicitly ask for a sign.

The most common tangible signs are finding small objects like feathers, coins, rocks, flowers, birds, rainbows and synchronistic meetings of people with information.

Birds are very common signs for many people when they are outside in nature, doing yard work or at their kitchen window. They will usually appear on Mother's Day, birthdays, anniversaries or the birth of a child. Always make note of the date when you experience a bird sign.

Red cardinal and **Blue Heron** symbolize a feminine presence, usually a sign from your mother, grandmother, sister, or aunt.

Hawks flying overhead symbolizes a male presence. A reminder that you are being protected. A positive affirmation for your project or a question. It is a symbol of freedom and flight for new ideas you may be working on.

Feathers signify honor, trust, strength, wisdom, power and freedom. It is a reminder of our connection to the spiritual realms and to divinity. Angels love to play with feathers. If you see feathers in an odd place or feel a feathery touch on your cheek, stop and acknowledge their presence.

Rainbows are one of the most beautiful spectacles nature has to offer. They are a sign of thank you, hope, or a promise of better times to come. A rainbow can be a sign of blessings for your venture. For some cultures, they are bridges between the worlds, a pathway leading to the light. Many outside funeral and memorial services end with a rainbow in a rainless sky.

Synchronistic information can come through people you just happen to meet, with a phone call, text or email from a friend or colleague. Life is meant to be shared with others.

We are never alone. Divine guidance and help are always available to us. It is so much fun to assemble a team to work together on a project. Ask your spiritual team for help and guidance on a project and then *trust* that it will come. Be open and allow the opportunities to come to you.

If you get stuck on a project, take a break and go outside for a walk or run an errand. Ask for helpful information to come through people you encounter along the way. Go out to local stores and see who you meet, notice license plates and signs on trucks.

They may have some very valuable information for you. Share with them what you are working on. Take a moment to talk to the friends or people you bump into. You will be surprised with the information and connections you will make. And it will be fun.

Life is easy when we lighten up and trust that the universe is abundant. Creation is actually a community creation. These messages can also come from your guardian angels or spirit guides.

Movement of Objects and Gentle Nudges

Missing keys or misplaced objects is a clear indication someone is trying to get your attention! It usually works, nothing is more frustrating than heading out the front door only to discover you don't have your keys. "Arrr"

Rather than get upset, acknowledge the interruption and be open to the guidance, as you search for your keys. Retrace the steps you took from the moment you came home. Pay attention to everything you see for clues. If they are not in this area, then look in the area you swear you did not enter, they are probably there.

Missing keys are usually done to slow you down or get your attention to bring something you will need later in the day.

Has this happened to you? Before leaving the house, you see an object or information and a thought crosses your mind to pick it up and bring it with you. It makes no sense why you would need it, so you ignore this nudge and go out the door.

Hours later this object has critical information for your meeting, and you don't have it. What an odd coincidence! Spirit or your higher self knew you would need it and was trying to alert you.

I am personally grateful to spirit for misplacing my keys and delaying my leaving the house by several minutes. It was a rainy dark night and the visibility was very poor. Just as I was accelerating onto the interstate, I had to stop suddenly to avoid a 5-car accident blocking the entire road.

It had just happened; people were still in their cars and the police had not arrived. I had to swerve my car to avoid hitting the cars, which were blocking all the lanes of travel. Fortunately, no one appeared to be seriously hurt, but all the cars were damaged and would need lengthy repair time.

Not something I had time for at that point in my life.

Seeing an Apparition

(Cloud of Smoke, Orbs in Photographs)

Seeing an apparition is an unusual or unexpected sight. The Catholic Church has reported apparitions of Mother Mary appearing to people to relay messages and expressing her ongoing motherly care for all the people on the earth. During the twentieth century, there have been 386 cases of Mary's apparition. Medjugorje, Lourdes and Fatima are some of the places Mother Mary has appeared with messages and healings. People have reported seeing Jesus, Mary and other religious figures in the room of sick or dying patients.

Colored orbs appear in the sky and can be captured in a photograph of a sunrise or a sunset. These can be nature spirits, energy beings or angels.

Deceased family members love to jump into our family photographs especially with children playing, holiday pictures, weddings and family reunions. They may appear as a round white orb or a large streak.

Orbs that appear in pictures of sunsets or sunrises may reflect the red, orange or green colors from the sun. Orbs in wedding photographs are becoming more common now with the use of digital camera phones.

Orbs are the curious translucent or solid circles (usually white) that appear unexpectedly in your photos. Orbs may appear in different sizes, as a single spot or as a multitude of spots grouped together. They are often proof of loved ones in Spirit, captured on film.

When these "Spirit Orbs" appear near a single person or group of people in a photo, it is a sign that your loved one is truly present and you are being blessed and loved. I share with you here a famous orb photograph from my daughter's wedding.

My husband Rick's presence was not only felt by the guests, but captured in this stunning photo of the bride dancing the father-daughter dance with her uncle Stephen. Notice the white orbs at the back of Stephen's head and in the middle of his back (larger on next page).

CHAPTER NINE

Angels

Spiritual Force of Angels
Waiting to Guide & Assist You

Angels are God's helpers. We are all given guardian angels at birth. They help us come into this world at birth, and they assist us during the transition process of our return home to the other side. They show us the way to be reunited with our loved ones in Spirit.

Our angels are with us to protect us and give us guidance. There are no limits to our angels' healing power. They can help us heal our relationships, career concerns, finances, housing issues, and any other challenge that is troubling us. They protect us from harm but they wait for us to ask for their help before they intervene. We all have free will to make our own choices.

"Ask and you shall receive." Angels love to have a job or a project. Lately, I have been in the habit of asking for a team of angels to help me with a project. (My team helped me write this book.) I said a special prayer to Archangel Gabriel everyday as I started my writing. Archangel

Gabriel is the great communicator. He assists writers, artists, and communicators with creative endeavors.

We just need to follow a few steps
to help the angels help us.

Ask. The Law of Free Will says that angels cannot intervene in our lives without our express permission. The only exception is if we are in a life-threatening situation, before it is our time to go.

Give the problem up to God. Let it go! Completely surrender the problem and know that it is taken care of. Abraham Hicks, a successful author and motivational speaker has a famous example of a woman asking her angels for help with a particular problem and then continuing to worry about it not happening. The angels get confused! They are only hearing her say the problem, so they continue to give her more of it. Worrying is a waste of time! Why would you give energy to something you don't want?

Trust in God's infinite wisdom and creativity to come up with a much better solution than our human minds could ever imagine.

Follow God's directions. After you release the problem to God and your angels, they may ask you to take some human steps to resolve the situation. These directions may come to you either in a voice, a dream, a vision, a knowingness, or an intuitive feeling. If you are unsure of the source of these messages, ask God for validation. Spiritual guidance will never be a fearful or hurtful.

You can ask your angels for guidance and use their help in your everyday life by asking for parking spaces, help with a new school, protecting a loved one on a trip or mission. You can give them a name and loan them out.

Parking Spaces

I have a dear friend who always asks her angels to help with finding parking spaces in busy parking lots. She always seems to be at the right place at the right time. A car will start to leave a front row spot just as she approaches. She always makes it a point to verbally thank her angels for this perfect parking spot. Amazing!

I always love when she offers to take her car to the crowded beach because I know we are assured a parking spot.

Special Angels Stay in the Family

This is nothing new, our ancestors were more in touch with their intuitive knowing and openly spoke about asking their angels for help. Some even gave their angels a name and would loan them out to relatives and grandchildren for special projects.

I sat next to a woman named Sara on a plane from Fort Myers to Baltimore recently. Her family has a guardian angel named Clarence. He was her grandfather's guardian angel that he would loan out or send to people who needed help.

He was so cherished that her grandfather gave Clarence to her aunt when he passed and her aunt has now passed him on to Sara.

She told me a story about her granddaughter Rachel calling her with concern and worry about her first day in a new middle school. She was very nervous about not knowing anyone and afraid she might get lost finding her classrooms in such a large building.

She asked if she could borrow Clarence for the day to help her.

Sara totally agreed and said, "Absolutely, I'll send him right over now to watch over you. Clarence will be on your left shoulder all day long. Don't forget to thank him at the end of the day and call me to let me know you are sending him back."

Sara called her granddaughter at the end of her first day and asked, "How was your day?" her granddaughter declared, "Oh Nana, it was so easy, I'm so glad I had Clarence with me. It was wonderful! I can give you Clarence back now."

Listen to Those Nudges

Sara received a frantic call from Travis, her husband's best friend. They had been best man at each other's weddings. His father had recently passed away, and he was trying to locate a special ring his father had given him years ago. He felt a connection to his father whenever he wore it.

He felt it was somewhere in the house, but had looked everywhere and could not find it. He was heartbroken to think it was lost forever. Sara thought a minute and just blunted out, "I'll send Clarence down to help you look!"

A week later Sara received a call from Travis. He told her about a big box in the garage that contained items his wife had set aside to donate to Good Will. Several times he thought he should check what she had put in it but discounted it. He trusted her decisions.

It was a nagging thought that continued until he finally decided to go and look through the contents of the box. He pulled everything out and there at the very bottom of the box was his father's ring.

Travis told Sara, "I believe Clarence has been trying to get me to go through that box for a week. I'm so glad I finally listened."

Aunt Loretta's Extra Guardian Angel

My Aunt Loretta was my godmother. She was an amazing woman, mother and grandmother. She always had kind words of wisdom and a smile on her face. You always felt safe and protected in her company. She raised five children and loved all of her 10 grandchildren. She maintained the wonderful tradition of Sunday dinner for her entire family. I remembered when Aunt Loretta gave her extra angel to her grandson, Ryan, when he was deployed to Iraq. I asked my cousin, Melanie Cherry, to tell her son Ryan's story and share her mother's angel prayer. This is Melanie's story.

I do not remember learning the Guardian Angel Prayer as a child. My mother probably taught it to me when I was very young. What I do remember is how protected and safe I felt each time I recited it.

Later in life, Mom told me about her "extra" Guardian Angel. She would reassure me that our loved-ones were safe because she was sending this Angel to accompany them on their journey, and I trusted that they would be protected and safe as well.

There is no doubt in my mind that Mom's extra Guardian Angel was with me when I moved to California with my husband. We were both 21. Joe was a Private First Class in the Marine Corps, and it was 1969. Mom's Angel worked overtime until our return to Rhode Island, when

Joe was being deployed to Southeast Asia. I know that Mom's Angel brought Joe back home to me, uninjured.

Mom's Angel was kept very busy throughout the years that followed: accompanying our family's children as they travelled the world, always bringing them home safely to us. My confidence in Divine Intervention had brought me far, and it would be put to the test in the years to come.

In May of 2000, Joe and I stood on the deck of Old Ironsides in Boston Harbor as our youngest son, Ryan, was commissioned as an officer in the Marine Corps. A few months later Ryan started Flight School. History was repeating itself.

September 11, 2001 began like most days, but as I watched the planes crash into the Twin Towers, I knew my life had changed. We were at war. My life would have been unbearable without my confidence in Mom's Angel to protect my family.

Ryan was deployed on two missions and came back safely. He was not supposed to have a third mission but he received orders to return to Iraq. The last time he saw his grandmother to say good-bye, she told him not to worry, he would return safely and she gifted him again her special Guardian Angel. I can only imagine how comforting this made him feel.

The months passed and my mother's health was failing. Visits to the nursing home were my daily routine. Ryan was still fighting in Iraq, and I was merely managing to put one foot in front of the other, on most days. The dreaded phone call came from my sister, Liz, that Mom had just passed to the Light. When I arrived at the nursing home, I hugged Liz and we both stood at Mom's bedside together, and my phone rang.

My husband Joe took my phone and left the room. He came right back and said, "It is Ryan, he wants to speak with you." Confused, I answered and asked him how he knew that Grammie had just died. He told me he was sorry about Grammie, but that he hadn't known. He was just calling to tell me that he was on his way home from Iraq. Knowing he was in a safe zone, he had just returned Grammie's Guardian Angel to her.

Even in death, Mom was leaving me with one final gift, one final hug. Mom was reminding me that her Angel would always be with me. I share with you, the reader, my mother's special Angel prayer.

Aunt Loretta's Angel Prayer

Angel of God, my guardian dear,
to whom God's love commits me here,
ever this day (or night) be at my side
to light and guard, to rule and guide.
Amen.

My cousin Melanie told me this story about Ryan's phone call when she called to inform me of my aunt's passing. "It gave me chills all down my spine." I knew my aunt had lingered in the nursing home for longer than the doctors had predicted, but I felt she was praying for Ryan to safely return home and return her Guardian Angel.

Remember our angels come in with us at birth and they help us on our journey home when we pass. Once Ryan was safe and on his way home, Aunt Lorretta's Guardian Angel returned to her to assist her on her final journey home.

Angels Hang Out in Airports!

This may sound strange to some people, but I LOVE to fly in airplanes. I have worn contact lenses since high school, so I knew I could never get my pilot's license; so instead, I let Southwest Airlines do the flying.

Over the years, I have had safe flights, but occasionally rough rides heading south in the winter during snow and ice storms. After my husband passed, I always felt I was closer to him when I was in an air, thirty-nine thousand feet closer, to be exact.

I traveled a lot with my daughters on vacation, so I would pray to him to watch over us and the airplane during the flight. I started to notice that all my flights were calm, on time or early even if we left late or the pilot would warn us to expect turbulence.

As I learned more about angels, I realized the pilot and co-pilot had guardian angels, so I made it a point to look out the window, while I was at the gate at the plane's cockpit. I usually can see them sitting in their seats, so I acknowledge their guardian angels on the left and right side of the two pilots and ask that they be protected and guided, during the flight. I always chuckle a little, as I imagine four angels with large wings inside that small cockpit.

Just as I board, I put my hand on the side of the plane and activate the plane's angels to watch over and protect this aircraft and all aircraft we encounter during this flight. At the end of the on-time smooth flight, I always thank the angels by tapping my hand on the side of the plane's body as I exit through the door. I always have the best flights.

I have met the most amazing people as my seat mates. I am somehow placed strategically with people who have a message for me or I can be of help to them with an encouraging uplifting message.

Orlando Airport Angels

I think angels hang out in airports, and I have met several of them over the years. I was in Orlando airport waiting for my departure flight and wanted to find a quiet spot to make a phone call. I was returning home after visiting my brother who had just been diagnosed with an incurable cancer. I found a deserted spot with comfortable chairs to make my call.

As I was talking, a man suddenly appeared out of nowhere and sat down beside me talking very loudly on his cellphone. I could hear him, and he could hear my conversation. All the other chairs were empty. Why did he have to sit so close to me?

He was trying to interrupt me to get my attention. I finally excused myself from my caller and asked him. "Can I help you?" He immediately said, "I overhead your conversation and felt compelled to talk to you. I was just recently diagnosed with cancer and have been researching the best hospitals in the country and found an excellent research hospital only an hour away. I have an appointment there tomorrow. Let me give you this information to give to your brother."

He truly was an angel sent to deliver this message for me to pass on to my brother.

That was my second Orlando airport angel story. In the first one, I was entering the tram, which is normally so crowded to go to the gate, when I noticed I was totally alone so, I picked a spot by the window with plenty of room. This never happens!

All of a sudden, an extremely handsome man with crystal blue eyes jumped on the tram and looked me straight in the eyes and asked if he could stand next to me. I agreed and we started small talk about why we were in Orlando.

He was on a business trip and I had been visiting my brother and his family. All of a sudden, he turned and said, "Oh, it's happening again! I am an angel and God gives me messages to give to people, when I fly. Your brother is going to be OK, please don't worry, he is going to be OK."

I was so shocked by his statement yet I could see in his eyes that it was a divine message from God that I was meant to pass on to my family. I thanked him and as we left the tram for our gate, we stopped and gave each other a big hug, not something I normally do to a total stranger, but it just seemed so natural, bidding goodbye to a dear friend.

I felt dizzy and a little dazed by this emotional meeting that I actually went down the wrong corridor and had to turn around and head in the other direction.

Just before I reached my gate, my blue-eyed angel jumped up all excited, his plane was leaving from the gate before mine. We proceeded to speak and share stories with each other for what seemed like an eternity. It felt like we were suspended in time.

He gave me a rosary prayer ring to give to my brother and I miraculously found an angel medal in my pocket that I gave to him. He mentioned that I could not mail his prayer ring to my brother, it had to be hand delivered, so I kept it in a safe place until my next visit.

A few weeks later, I received a call from my brother's son-in-law Dave. He was visiting his parents in Rhode Island and would love to meet me for lunch. This was perfect, I could tell Dave the angel story and have him deliver the rosary prayer ring to my brother. I wrapped the prayer ring in a small felt bag for safe keeping and put it in my pocketbook.

I was not quite sure how to tell Dave my blue-eyed angel story and how he would relay it to my brother. I have to admit, I was thinking. "My family is going to think I am nuts!"

I felt a little more at ease after Dave shared with me, he had recently been certified in the healing modality of Reiki, so I knew he understood the healing power of energy and prayer.

I took the small bag out and laid it on the table in front of us and started to tell my story.

I noticed Dave's eyes were very wide with wonder and disbelief, as small white feathers appeared in the bag and all around the ring. The more I pulled out, more appeared, it was endless. They looked like angel feathers.

The two of us realized had we both not been there together to witness it, we would not have believed it. You can't make this stuff up!

I received a phone call from my sister-in-law after Dave returned home and gave my brother the rosary prayer ring. They were really surprised and pleased to hear the story and specially to see the pictures of the abundance of feathers overflowing from the bag.

This rosary prayer ring brought my brother great comfort and he cherished it by carrying it in his pocket every day.

STOP! STOP!

We have a team in the higher realms who watch over us and provide us with guidance and support along our journey. Some may call them guiding angels, spirit guides, God, ascended masters, teachers, or departed loved ones.

Yes, our departed loved ones continue to send us their love and guidance from the other side. They intervene when they see us going the wrong way or headed for an accident.

One of my first encounters with this type of intervention was when I was 17 years old. I had taken my father's brand-new car to the local store.

It was a beautiful sunny day and I was playing the radio very loud and singing along to the music thinking I was so cool driving this fancy new car, when suddenly, out of the blue, I heard a loud voice scream, "STOP" "STOP!"

I must have unconsciously put my foot on the brake because I heard a screeching sound, I felt the car stop abruptly, and I felt a force on my body pulling me back.

It all happened so fast, my eyes were not registering the actual moment. When I jolted back into reality, I saw the entire hood of my father's new car under the back end of a very large oil truck. The end of the truck was up to my windshield. It was surreal! I sat stunned, not knowing if I was alive or dead, and thinking my father was going to kill me for damaging his car.

Miraculously, when the light turned green, the truck was able to pull forward over the hood of the car, leaving the car unscratched and me unharmed.

I don't know whose voice that was that yelled at me to STOP, but I thanked them profusely for saving my life. Cars did not have seat belts until the late 1960's so the force I felt pulling my body back protected me like a seat belt. I assumed it was my guardian angel protecting me from a horrific accident. It was not my destiny to be involved in a terrible accident that day, and I'm so glad I listened to that voice within telling me to hit the brakes and stop the car.

Angels will intervene to save us from our mistakes if it goes against our path of destiny.

You are here in this physical form with a sacred soul purpose to help mankind. It has been said by many masters that we each have a unique gift that only we can bring to the earth at this time.

****

CHAPTER TEN

Relationships

The Positive or Negative Affect
on our Lives

The Infinity Sign of 8 is known in numerology as the number of balance and alignment. It symbolizes the ability of bringing heaven onto the earth. A place of peace, it is actually our natural state of alignment with Spirit.

We can reach this state when we pray, sit in meditation, take a walk on the beach, in nature, or with people we love. You can feel this alignment in your heart.

This balanced state calms your mind, slows your heart rate and allows your body to relax and rejuvenate. It teaches us to feel with our hearts what feels right or wrong with a particular situation we may be facing.

We all have an inner voice, silently guiding us. The key is to take the time to *listen*. When we are undecided about a question, we have about a life situation; we may know what we want, but we factor in everybody else's desires and wishes. Many times, we are not being truthful about our real feelings. This is not always the best thing for us and others.

Next time you are invited to an event, wait to give your acknowledgment. Stop and think about it. How does it make you feel?

Your gut instinct never lies. Are you excited or is there a sense of dread? Do you have the time to attend? If the answer is no, be honest and respectfully decline the invitation. You will be amazed how wonderful it will feel. You have honored your intuitive guidance.

It is so important to be honest with ourselves about how we feel about a particular situation. We all deserve and respect honesty. It is not always easy being honest and expressing our feelings to others, especially people we love, but in the long run it works best for all concerned. We cannot live by others wants or needs, if we do, we are not following our intuition and soul's path.

We are connected energetically to each other and all living things through vibrations. It is all about vibration. We are in a higher vibration when we are happy, joyful and feeling loved. Our vibrational energy is low when we are fearful, angry, feeling unworthy or sad.

Many times, other people can affect our vibrational energy field when we are with them for a period of time. If someone we work or live with is negative, angry or critical, we will be affected by their negativity.

It is best to stay away from lower vibrational people, as much as possible. You know the old saying, one rotten apple spoils the entire basket of healthy apples.

Here is an easy exercise to determine who makes you feel joyful and who drains you of your energy.

Listing Energy Drains in Your Life

On a blank sheet of paper draw a line down the middle to make two columns. Mark a **+Positive** heading on the left column and a **−Negative** heading column on the right column across the top of the paper.

Throughout the course of your day make note of *how you feel after* everyone you physically come into contact with in person, on the phone, or through text, social media, and emails. If you feel happy, joyful, or uplifted, then write their name in the positive column. If you feel sad, despair, or anger, then write their name in the negative column.

Do this exercise for a week or more, and you will start to see a pattern develop. Make note of everyone you have on your +Positive list. These people and places are your vibrational matches, and you need to spend more time with them growing and developing your creative ideas.

The minuses, the −Negative group, are not in your vibration and are a drain on your energy. Limit the time you spent with them.

Weekly Chart of Feelings	
+ POSITIVE	− NEGATIVE

If they are family members call on your guardian angels to protect you, while you are speaking with them or being in their presence. After you leave, state your desire to disengage your energy from them. Try to think of the positive aspects of this family member and send them love to reinforce their positive attributes.

We are not alone. We are connected to each other through vibrations. Have you ever been thinking of someone and suddenly the phone rings and it is that person calling you? You were both connecting energetically, and one of you was drawn to make the call. Interesting how connected we all are.

Is it Time to Say Good Bye?

This year and a half has been a very difficult time for everyone. Many people who are currently in short and long-term relationships are starting to question, "Is this relationship right for me? We have had many wonderful fun times together, but we are not on the same path anymore." Is your spouse or partner coming up on your –Negative chart, to show you, they are not a vibrational match for you?

What do you do? You have a lot invested in this relationship. You may have children, a life you built together, but now it all feels so distant. You may feel you have nothing in common except your kids. If this sounds like you and your life, don't ignore this nudge. It is your intuition speaking to you. It is reminding you to take more time for yourself and reflect on what you need and want.

Are your needs being met? If not, then start now to open up the dialogue with your partner. Be honest with each other about how you *really feel* about x, y, z.

We are not the same people we were ten or twenty years ago. What brings you joy? Are you getting enough free time to follow your dreams and creative endeavors? If not, what can you suggest to change it?

Maybe it is time to rewrite the owner's manual. It can be fun re-designing it together. The key is to be honest with yourself and with each other.

****

CHAPTER ELEVEN

Trust It!

You Have the Power Within

In this book I have shared with you knowledge and gifts I learned at an early age through a Near-Death Experience (NDE). I learned not be afraid. I was not alone! We are never alone, and that fear was only a temporary illusion.

There was always loving help and support available to me from my eternal family. At the time, I was unaware that this loving support was coming to me from my heavenly family. All I felt was unconditional love.

It taught me to intuitively trust my inner knowingness. I was able to feel in my heart when something felt right or wrong and I learned this inner guidance was always available to me any time, day or night.

I describe my Near-Death Experience in detail in my first book, ***Believe in Forever: How to Recognize Signs from Departed Loved Ones***. I will summarize the lessons I and my family learned from my experience.

- I retained a sense of knowingness and a sixth sense to receive communication from my family in heaven.
- I learned to trust my own inner guidance or intuition. I found it never failed me.
- I became aware that I did not have a sense of fear like other children.
- I always felt the answers were available to me, if I asked for help.

This helped me tremendously as I was growing up. I would always follow my hunches. If I was invited to go somewhere and it did not feel right to me, I would ask myself, is this the best thing for me to do? I would sit quietly and feel with my heart. If I got an uneasy feeling, I would decline the invitation.

Over time, I noticed my hunches were always right, so I realized that fearing something was a waste of time. Worrying is also a waste of time and carries a lower vibration. We need to stay in a higher vibration to access higher guidance.

Years later, my mother shared with me just how sick I had been and how the doctors had prepared my parents that I may not live or could suffer some permanent damage. She also told me that she did not believe the doctors, she just knew I was going to be all right. She had not allowed herself to go into fear and worry about the "what if." She continued to remain positive about my recovery.

I learned at an early age to not go into fear. Unconditional love and support are always available to us. All we need to do is ask and the guidance will be given. This lack of fear is what I believe made me a survivor of my Near-Death Experience. I share this knowledge of accessing intuitive guidance through signs and synchronicities with you, the reader, to help you on this journey we call life.

I pray this book has offered you some

enlightenment to trust your inner voice.

Use this knowledge to go within and

listen to your heart. It has been there all along,

just waiting for you to listen.

Be open to the signs and synchronicities that come your

way and acknowledge them with gratitude.

May you have the courage of the lion to speak your truth

and manifest your soul's desire.

May God bless you on this wonderful journey we call life.

Love & Light,

Mary Catherine

About the Author

 Mary Catherine Volk is a best-selling author, spiritual advisor, and speaker. She serves as an ambassador between the worlds. Her teachings are filled with inspiration, empowerment, and love. Since a Near-Death Experience at the age of six, Mary was given the gift of knowing that life exists beyond this physical realm, that life is eternal, and we always have access to divine guidance. That became the topic of Mary's first book, *Believe in Forever: How to Recognize Signs from Departed Loved Ones*.

In this new book, *Trust It! You Have the Power Within You*, Mary takes her years of experience to speak about the issues we are all facing since the Covid-19 pandemic. She has noticed the tremendous fear in people and knows that fear causes a lower vibration which is the exact opposite of where you need to be to access your intuitive guidance. With every thought and word, you emit a frequency that has a positive or negative effect. Be a master of your words! Bless a situation rather than criticize it.

This latest book teaches techniques to align your vibration with the higher realms. There are infinite possibilities when you think from a high vibrational state of joy, gratitude and love. Create a life of endless possibilities. Your guardian angels, spirit guides, ascended masters, teachers, and loved ones in Spirit are all ready to assist.

As a shamanic practitioner, Mary Catherine founded a specialized modality for releasing emotional blockages from present day, past lives, and inherited ancestral emotional traumas. It empowers the client to make life choices that align with their joy and soul purpose.

She has studied with internationally known shaman don Oscar Miro-Quesada, Eric Dowsett and spiritual medium James Van Praagh. She conducts workshops and has been the guest speaker at holistic expos, IANDS Conferences, and on radio and television shows.

Mary Catherine Volk lives by the beach in Narragansett, Rhode Island and visits regularly with her family and grandchildren in Texas. She loves the outdoors, nature, art, theater, spirituality, and living a joyful life with family and friends.

www.MaryCatherineVolk.com

www.facebook.com/marycatherine.volk.3

Made in the USA
Middletown, DE
27 May 2021

40553673R00066